WHEN BODY LANGUAGE GOES BAD

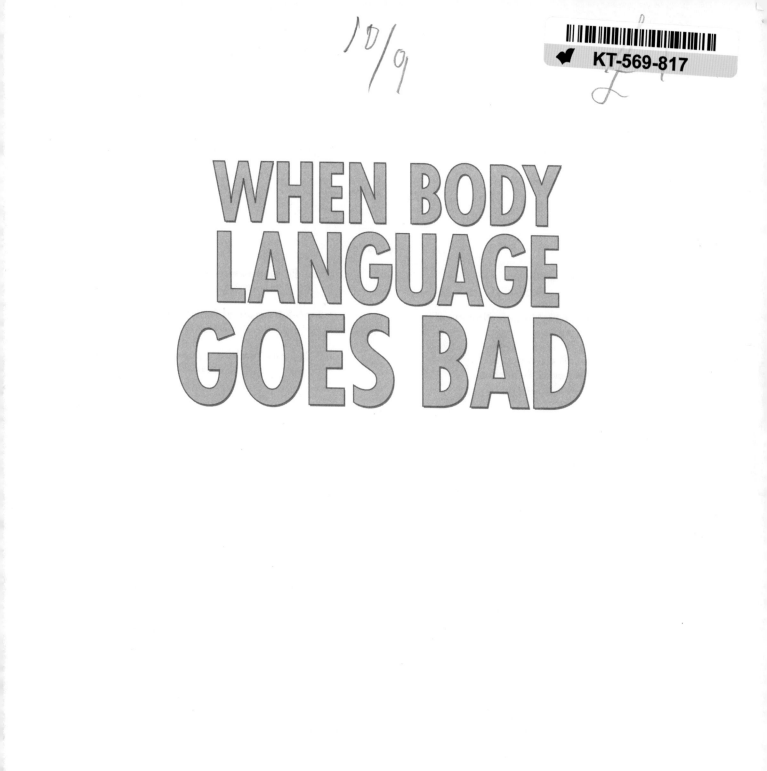

Other DILBERT books from Boxtree

Business Books

The Dilbert Principle
TPB ISBN: 0-7522-2470-0
PB ISBN: 0-7522-7220-9

The Way of the Weasel
ISBN: 0-7522-6503-2

The Dilbert Fortune
TPB ISBN: 0-7522-1161-7
PB ISBN: 0-7522-7221-7

Dogbert's Top Secret Management Handbook
ISBN: 0-7522-1148-X

The Joy of Work
TPB ISBN: 0-7522-1720-8
PB ISBN: 0-7522-7222-5

Treasuries

Fugitive From the Cubicle Police
ISBN: 0-7522-2431-X

Seven Years of Highly Defective People
ISBN: 0-7522-2407-7

What Do you Call a Sociopath in a Cubicle? Answer: A Coworker
ISBN: 0-7522-2417-4

When did Ingnorance Become a Point of View?
ISBN: 0-7522-2412-3

Dilbert–A Treasury of Sunday Strips: Version 00
ISBN: 0-7522-7232-2

It's Obvious You Won't Survive By Your Wits Alone
ISBN: 0-7522-0201-4

Collections

Excuse Me While I Wag
ISBN: 0-7522-2399-2

Dilbert Gives You the Business
ISBN: 0-7522-2394-1

Journey to Cubeville
ISBN: 0-7522-2384-4

Build a Better Life by Stealing Office Supplies
ISBN: 0-7522-0716-4

Shave the Wales
ISBN: 0-7522-0849-7

Bring Me the Head of Willy the Mailboy!
ISBN: 0-7522-0136-0

Dogbert's Clues for the Clueless
ISBN: 0-7522-0711-3

Another Day in Cubicle Paradise
ISBN: 0-7522-2486-7

Random Acts of Management
ISBN: 0-7522-7174-1

Don't Step in the Leadership
ISBN: 0-7522-2389-5

I'm Not Anti-Business, I'm Anti-Idiot
ISBN: 0-7522-2379-8

Casual Day Has Gone Too Far
ISBN: 0-7522-1119-6

Still Pumped from Using the Mouse
ISBN: 0-7522-2265-1

Always Postpose Meetings with Time-Wasting Morons
ISBN: 0-7522-0854-3

Best of Dilbert

The Best of Dilbert Volume 1
ISBN: 0-7522-6541-5

Best of Dilbert Volume 2
ISBN: 0-7522-1500-0

For ordering information, call 01625 677237

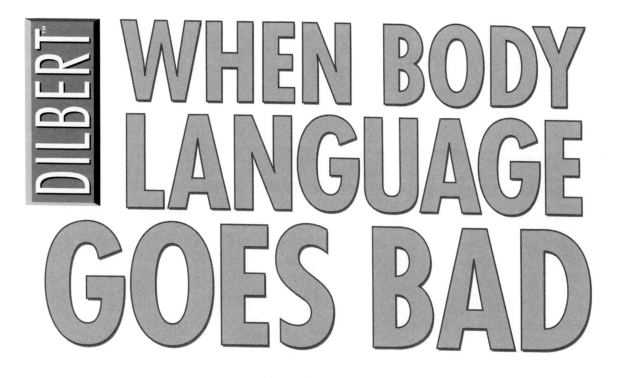

DILBERT™

WHEN BODY LANGUAGE GOES BAD

A DILBERT™ BOOK
BY SCOTT ADAMS

BXTREE

First published 2003 by Andrews McMeel Publishing, an Andrews McMeel Universal company,
4520 Main Street, Kansas City, Missouri 64111, USA

First published in Great Britain 2003 by Boxtree
an imprint of Pan Macmillan Ltd
Pan Macmillan, 20 New Wharf Road, London N1 9RR
Basingstoke and Oxford
Associated companies throughout the world
www.panmacmillan.com

ISBN 0 7522 2491 3

DILBERT® is a registered trademark of United Feature Syndicate, Inc.

DOGBERT and DILBERT appear in the comic strip DILBERT®, distributed by United Feature Syndicate, Inc.

www.dilbert.com

9 8 7 6 5 4 3 2 1

A CIP catalogue record for this book is available from the British Library

Printed by The Bath Press Ltd, Bath

For Lodi's best product

Introduction

My body speaks several languages and that's not counting the stuff that comes out of my mouth. For example, my knees speak the African clicking language for the first few hours after I wake up. It's a sarcastic sound and I assume they are mocking me. I plan to record it someday and have it translated, as soon as I can find the African clicking embassy.

My face likes to send messages that are wholly independent from my brain. Sometimes my brain will be thinking a happy thought such as "I like cookies" while my face is saying, "I buried a salesman in my basement." This phenomenon worsens when I'm deep in thought. I'll be mentally writing my next hilarious *Dilbert* episode in my head while wandering around at the mall and the next thing I know children are screaming and the townspeople are gathering torches. That, along with the fact that my clothing size is pi, is why I hate shopping.

Needless to say, I am what you might call "unapproachable." I have been going to the same gym for the past ten years and no stranger has ever tried to start a conversation with me. Part of the problem is that when I lift anything heavier than a cotton ball I contort my face as if someone had just driven a railroad spike through my thigh. And on the odd occasion where I initiate conversation—say to ask if a piece of equipment is available—I am handicapped by a severe propensity to mumble. I can overcome the mumbling after I get warmed up, but because I work at home, I often go for hours with no human contact. So my first few words after a silent stretch always come off sounding like a demonic threat.

Me: "Are you done with that piece of equipment?"

What they hear: "I will disembowel you and send your soul to the Dark Region!"

Luckily, both interpretations give me immediate and unlimited use of the equipment. I guess I can't complain.

Another thing I can't complain about is that there's still time to join Dogbert's New Ruling Class (DNRC) and be by his side when he conquers the world and makes everyone else our domestic servants. To be a member all you need to do is sign up for the free *Dilbert Newsletter* that is published approximately whenever I feel like it—about five times a year if you're lucky.

To subscribe or unsubscribe, go to www.dilbert.com. If you have problems with the automated subscription method, write tonewsletter@unitedmedia.com.

S.Adams

Scott Adams

14

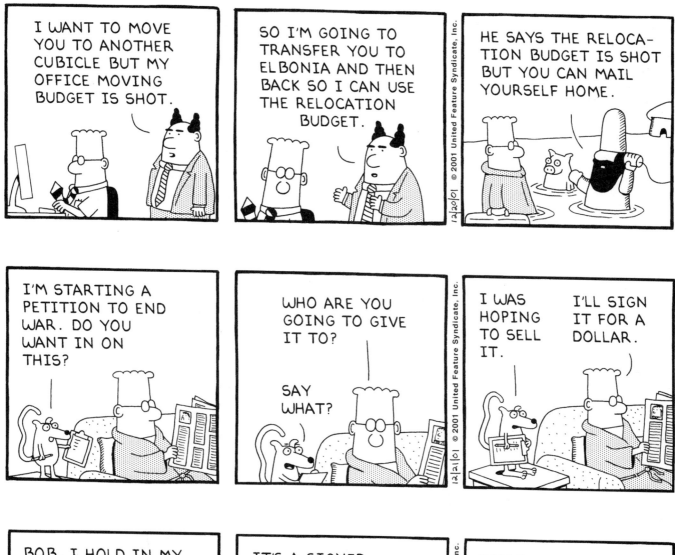

32

36

40

41

44

61

62

65

68

85

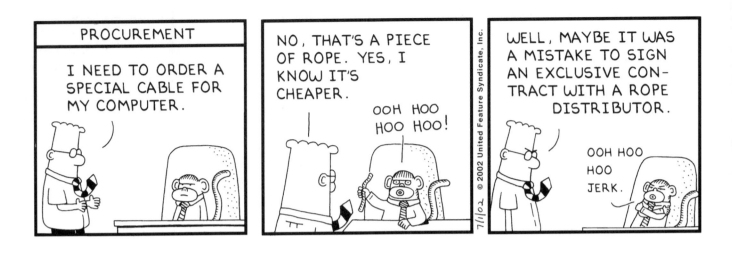

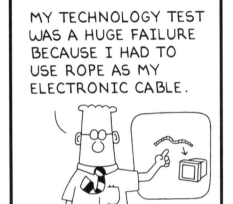

Panel 1: DO YOU THINK I SHOULD INJECT A DEADLY POISON IN MY FACE TO HIDE WRINKLES?

Panel 2: IT'S ONLY FAIR THAT YOU POISON YOUR FACE, BECAUSE YOUR FACE IS KILLING ME. HEE HEE HEE!

Panel 3: THE CORRECT ANSWER IS "YOU DON'T NEED TO."

WAS YOUR MOTHER A SHAR-PEI?

Panel 4: OVER THE PAST YEAR, MOST OF MY CO-WORKERS HAVE MANAGED EXPENSIVE PROJECTS THAT FAILED.

Panel 5: I'VE DONE NOTHING BUT DRINK COFFEE. SO ON AN ECONOMIC BASIS, THAT MAKES ME YOUR TOP PERFORMER.

Panel 6: WATCH AND LEARN.

Panel 7: HOW'S YOUR NEW BABY?

Panel 8: WONDERFUL, BUT THE LACK OF SLEEP IS TAKING A TOLL ON MY BODY.

Panel 9: HOW'S BECKY DOING?

I AM BECKY. BOB LOOKS WORSE.

122

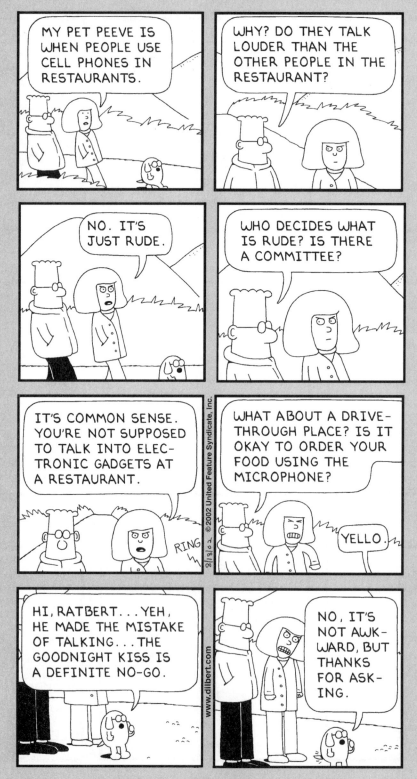